NATIVE AMERICAN ART

FROM TOTEMS TO TEXTILES

BY JOAN STOLTMAN

Gareth Stevens
PUBLISHING

Please visit our website, www.garethstevens.com. For a free color catalog of all our high-quality books, call toll free 1-800-542-2595 or fax 1-877-542-2596.

Library of Congress Cataloging-in-Publication Data

Names: Stoltman, Joan, author.
Title: Native American art : from totems to textiles / Joan Stoltman.
Description: New York : Gareth Stevens Publishing, [2018] | Series: Native
  American cultures | Includes index.
Identifiers: LCCN 2017026588| ISBN 9781538208724 (pbk.) | ISBN 9781538208731 (6 pack) | ISBN
9781538208748 (library bound)
Subjects: LCSH: Indian art–North America–Juvenile literature. | Indians of
  North America–Material culture–Juvenile literature.
Classification: LCC E98.A7 S83 2018 | DDC 704.03/97–dc23
LC record available at https://lccn.loc.gov/2017026588

First Edition

Published in 2018 by
Gareth Stevens Publishing
111 East 14th Street, Suite 349
New York, NY 10003

Copyright © 2018 Gareth Stevens Publishing

Designer: Sarah Liddell
Editor: Therese Shea

Photo credits: Cover, p. 1 (main image) poemnist/Shutterstock.com; cover, p. 1 (right totem pole) StockWithMe/Shutterstock.com; cover, p. 1 (weaver) Junkyardsparkle/Wikimedia Commons; cover, p. 1 (tapestry) Tillman/Wikimedia Commons; pp. 4, 21 (main) US National Archives bot/ Wikimedia Commons; p. 5 Harvey Meston/Staff/Archive Photos/Getty Images; pp. 7, 11, 15 (main) Werner Forman/Contributor/Universal Images Group/Getty Images; p. 8 Jbarta/Wikimedia Commons; p. 9 Peter Unger/Lonely Planet Images/Getty Images; p. 12 Daderot/Wikimedia Commons; p. 13 Myrabella/Wikimedia Commons; p. 15 (seed beads) Stephen Jingel/Shutterstock.com; p. 17 Rotatebot/Wikimedia Commons; p. 18 Phyzome/Wikimedia Commons; pp. 19, 23 (Lucy Telles and Nellie Charlie) Cullen328/Wikimedia Commons; pp. 21 (Clara Sherman), 23 (Delores E. Churchill) FastilyClone/Wikimedia Commons; p. 23 (Mike Dart) Whitekiller/Wikimedia Commons; p. 23 (Kelly Jean Church) Uyvsdi/Wikimedia Commons; p. 25 Jack Mitchell/Contributor/Archive Photos/ Getty Images; p. 27 Glenn Asakawa/Contributor/Denver Post/Getty Images; p. 29 (Chilkat blanket) Coat of Many Colors/Wikimedia Commons; p. 29 (bracelets) Silverborders/Wikimedia Commons; p. 29 (watercolor) Josiemock/Wikimedia Commons; p. 29 (Kachina dolls) Kaitlyn153/ Wikimedia Commons; p. 29 (sand painting) OgreBot/Wikimedia Commons.

Printed in the United States of America

CPSIA compliance information: Batch #CW18GS: For further information contact Gareth Stevens, New York, New York at 1-800-542-2595.

CONTENTS

Words in the glossary appear in **bold** type the first time they are used in the text.

WHAT IS ART?

Many people see art as a way of recording and presenting a story, thought, or belief. Artists design, or plan the look of, a piece and then create it with certain **materials**. Today, artists may be hired by someone to make their art.

Many Native Americans don't think of art like this. Art is a part of life. Art might be clothing, food jars, or **religious** pieces. Art objects are to be touched and used. Native men, women, and children made art in the past—and still do today!

NATIVE AMERICAN STUDENT-ARTISTS' WEAVING AND BEAD PROJECTS

When Europeans first came to North America, many Native American languages didn't have words for "art" or "artist."

USEFUL ART

Native American art isn't a single style. Every community has its own history, **culture**, and designs. Not all Native American groups make the same kinds of objects. Some are known for baskets, while others make pottery. Some mastered masks, while others are famous for blankets.

Most Native American art has one thing in common: It's used for something. Some art is made to speak with spirits or gods. Other art tells stories. Pottery for cooking can be art, too. There's no limit to art's uses.

DID YOU KNOW?

Respect for nature is important in native art. Haudenosaunee (or Iroquois) artists may speak to a tree before they begin carving, or cutting into, its wood.

6

In Native American art, **symbols** are meant to show
the spirit of their subject, not what it really looks like.
Why? Only the Creator God can make things perfectly.

ANCIENT ART

Native American art covers everything from 10,000-year-old pottery to modern paintings. It's hard to say anything that would apply to every piece of art!

There are many questions remaining about ancient native art. We often don't know who made certain objects or what they were used for. Ancient symbols may not mean what we think they do. Things made from wood or wool break down over time, so we may not even know if we have the whole work of art!

ANCIENT PECOS CERAMIC BOWL

DID YOU KNOW?

Much of what we know about ancient cultures comes from finding pieces of pottery. Pottery can survive for thousands of years.

There's a history behind ancient native art—but we often don't know what that history is! These rock carvings at Puerco Pueblo, Arizona, were created around AD 1300.

9

CHANGING ART

Some kinds of native art changed over time. Other art forms were lost completely. For example, peoples of the Southeast were once known for great stone carvings. This art is no longer practiced, though wood carving has replaced it.

Questions remain about native art that isn't so ancient, too. That's because many native peoples, including some Eastern Woodland communities, died of disease brought by Europeans. Others were killed or forced from their homelands. While they were fighting for their survival, their **traditional** art suffered.

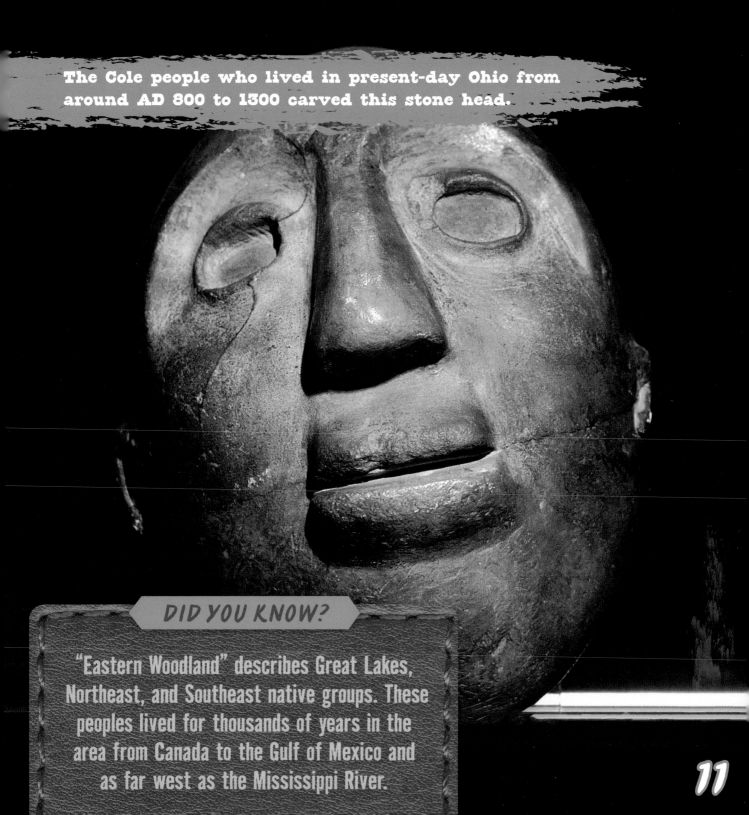

The Cole people who lived in present-day Ohio from around AD 800 to 1300 carved this stone head.

DID YOU KNOW?

"Eastern Woodland" describes Great Lakes, Northeast, and Southeast native groups. These peoples lived for thousands of years in the area from Canada to the Gulf of Mexico and as far west as the Mississippi River.

MAKING MASKS

Masks show the huge range in Native American art. Many groups have made masks for religious events since ancient times. Navajo masks are made of leather. The Cherokee make masks from dried **gourds**. The Inuit carve small finger masks from wood that dancers wear on their hands.

Hopi kachina masks are considered to be living spirits. They're so **sacred** that only certain people can bring them to and from events. They can never be sold.

INUIT FINGER MASK

DID YOU KNOW?

Haudenosaunee "False Face" masks are made from dried cornhusks and the wood of a live tree. They can't be drawn, photographed, or displayed because they're sacred.

Transformation masks are still made today by groups along the Northwest Coast. When these wood masks are opened, they have a second face carved inside!

ART WITH PORCUPINE QUILLS!

In the Great Plains, making art was part of everyday life. Even so, Cheyenne and Lakota artists were valued just as much as warriors, or fighters. Quillwork was one art for which these Native Americans were known.

For quillwork, porcupine quills were dyed, softened, and then flattened, folded, twisted, wrapped, and sewn, usually onto leather or bark. Quill artists could only be skilled women who took part in quillwork societies. Each woman's quill designs were her personal property and couldn't be copied.

DID YOU KNOW?

Quillwork was a very sacred art and sometimes even a form of prayer. Quillwork was almost lost forever, but a few people still practice it today.

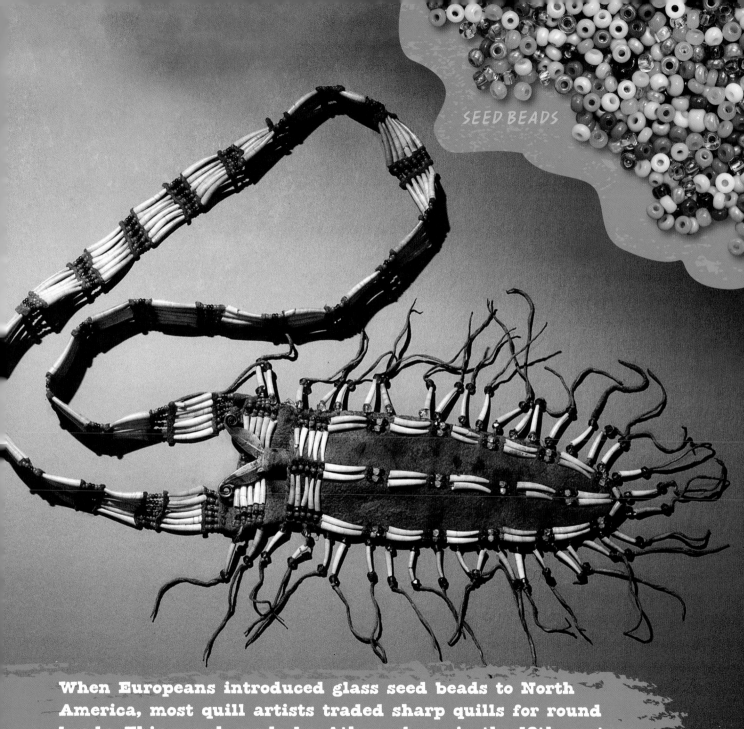

SEED BEADS

When Europeans introduced glass seed beads to North America, most quill artists traded sharp quills for round beads. This pouch made by Athapaskans in the 18th century is decorated with both quills and glass beads.

TOTEM POLES OF THE NORTHWEST COAST

Pacific Northwest peoples traded with each other for thousands of years. Later, trade with Europeans meant great wealth for natives such as the Tlingit and Haida. Rich natives became interested in buying art. Some in their communities became **professional** artists.

Totem poles were one form of art in this area. Early totem poles were small enough to carry. In the late 1700s, Europeans introduced metal tools. These were used to construct totem poles as tall as 40 feet (12 m)! The symbols, colors, and stories told through the poles were the same, though.

DID YOU KNOW?

Totem poles existed long before Europeans came to North America. However, since the totem poles were made of wood, they haven't survived to present day.

TOTEM POLES
IN THUNDERBIRD PARK
(BRITISH COLUMBIA, CANADA)

Traditionally, a totem pole shows a family's history and its link to spirits. You could "read" a family's totem pole to get to know them!

17

CLAY CREATIVITY

In the Southwest, almost all ancient arts still continue today. Native peoples there weren't forced to leave their lands and survive elsewhere. This allowed them to practice and pass on their culture and skills.

Pueblo pottery is one of the most famous of all native arts. It's made the same as it was 1,000 years ago. Paintbrushes are still made from chewing leaves of the yucca plant! Each Pueblo group—including the Hopi, Acoma, Santa Clara, and Zuni—has its own style of pottery.

CERAMIC JAR BY NAMPEYO

DID YOU KNOW?

Pueblo pottery was traditionally made by only women. Daughters and granddaughters were taught how to dig and clean clay, make dyes, and shape pottery. Secret clay locations were passed down!

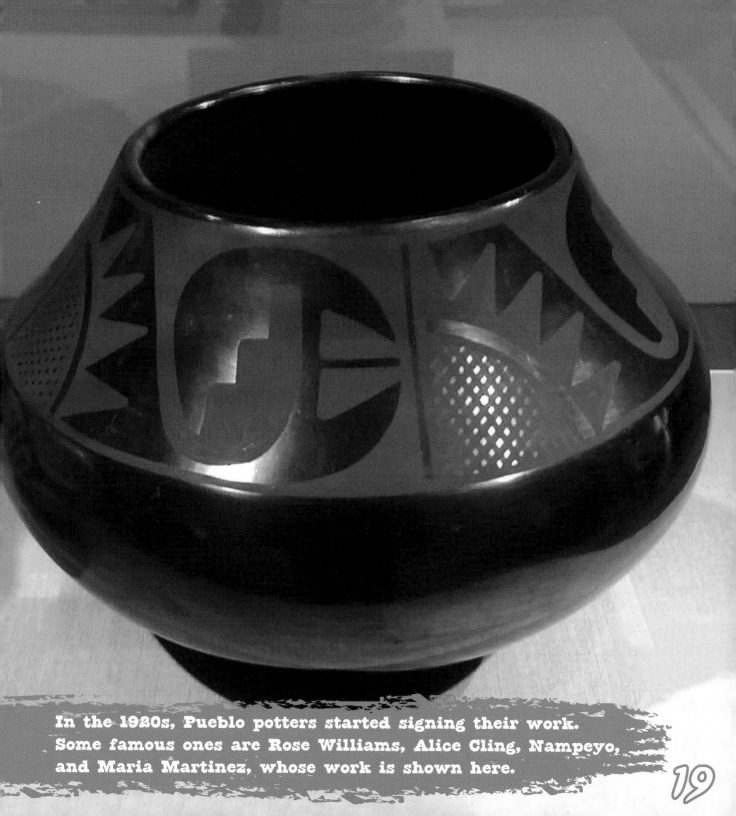

In the 1920s, Pueblo potters started signing their work. Some famous ones are Rose Williams, Alice Cling, Nampeyo, and Maria Martinez, whose work is shown here.

19

WONDERFUL WOVEN WORK

The Navajo are the best-known **weavers** of the Native Americans of North America. The Navajo came to the Southwest in the 10th and 11th centuries. No one knows if they knew how to weave then. If they didn't, they quickly learned the skills and designs of the nearby Pueblo peoples—and soon were more famous than their teachers!

Native weavers make and dye yarn. They often make their own looms, the main tool used to weave. Because it takes months to create a rug or blanket, weaving is a part of daily life.

DID YOU KNOW?

Blankets, rugs, and other **textiles** were made from cotton until the Spanish brought sheep to the area. It takes the wool of two or three sheep to make a 3-foot-by-5-foot (1 m by 1.5 m) rug!

Like Great Plains quillwork, Navajo weaving can be an act of prayer.

LABELING NATIVE ART

In 1935, the US government created the Indian Arts and Crafts Board to help Native Americans make money through their art. Because fakes were being sold, the board created rules about who could label their goods "Indian made" to help actual Native American artists sell their art.

However, the board often allowed only traditional art to be labeled. It didn't allow anything with modern style. It also left out artists from native groups that had been **disbanded** or from "tribes, bands, or nations" that weren't recognized by the US government.

FAMOUS NATIVE AMERICAN BASKET WEAVERS

DELORES E. CHURCHILL
HAIDA

LUCY TELLES
MONO LAKE PAIUTE-KUCADIKADI
AND SOUTHERN SIERRA MIWOK

NELLIE CHARLIE
MONO LAKE PAIUTE-KUCADIKADI

MIKE DART
CHEROKEE

KELLY JEAN CHURCH
GRAND TRAVERSE BAND OF OTTAWA AND OJIBWE

Basketry, or weaving natural materials into a basket, is one of the great traditional arts.

MEET A MODERN ARTIST

Just because an artist is Native American doesn't mean they have to work in traditional arts. Some artists find traditional arts limiting. Their work is about their community's culture, traditions, and history, but it doesn't look like the art of the past.

James Luna is one of the most famous artists working today. He's won many awards for his art. His art isn't traditional at all! He's known for a newer type of art called performance art, in which an event planned by an artist happens in front of people.

DID YOU KNOW?

In the performance piece *Take a Picture with a Real Indian*, James Luna dressed as a Plains warrior. People walking by wanted a photo with him. He later changed into pants and a shirt. No one wanted a photo with him. What do you think this piece means?

JAMES LUNA, LUISEÑO

James Luna is one of a few Native Americans today whose pieces are in major art museums.

25

WHERE CAN YOU SEE IT?

One of the biggest problems Native American art has faced is how to display it. In years past, pieces from different communities and time periods were placed together at natural history museums. The meaning of a piece in its original community was left out.

Even when this art was moved to art museums, it was placed with art from other ancient native cultures and labeled as "**primitive**." This treatment unfairly makes Native American art seem less cultured and less artistic than the art of other peoples.

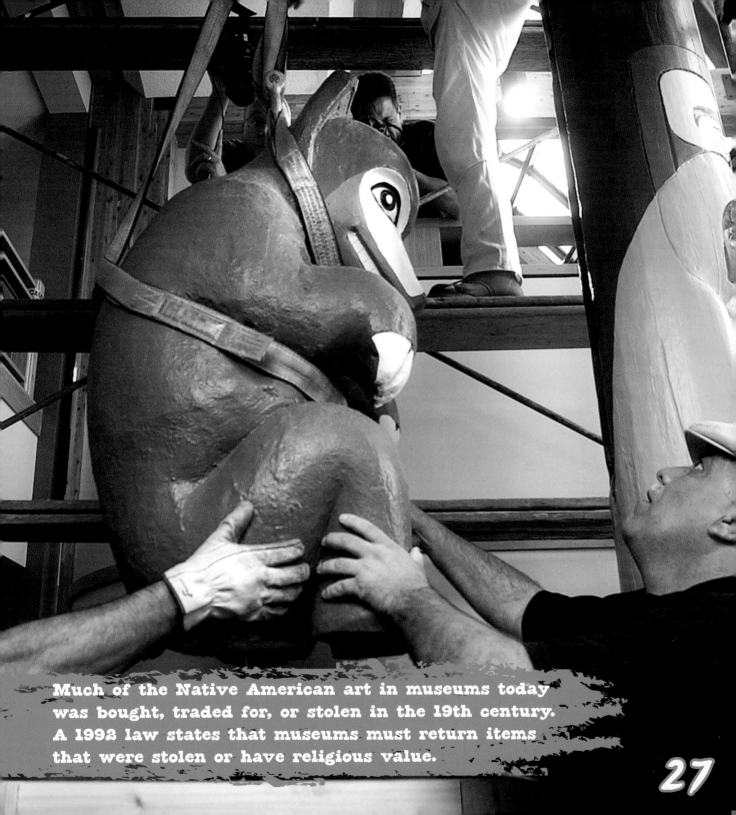

Much of the Native American art in museums today was bought, traded for, or stolen in the 19th century. A 1992 law states that museums must return items that were stolen or have religious value.

SO MUCH MORE!

It's impossible to include all kinds of Native American art from thousands of years in one book. With more than 550 federally recognized tribes, 225 nonrecognized tribes, and communities that no longer exist, there are more styles of art than anyone could ever count!

Haida artist Robert Davidson explains art's importance to native peoples: "Art was our only written language. . . . Throughout our history, it has been the art that has kept our spirit alive." Learning about Native American art helps keep their history alive, too.

AN ABUNDANCE OF OTHER ARTS

CHILKAT BLANKETS

SILVER JEWELRY OF THE NAVAJO, ZUNI, KEWA (SANTO DOMINGO), AND HOPI

PUEBLO AND PLAINS WATERCOLORS

HOPI KACHINA DOLLS

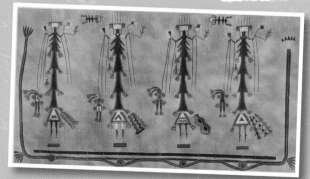

NAVAJO SANDPAINTING

These are just some of the many amazing art forms that weren't covered in this book. Ask an adult to help you learn more at the library or online.

GLOSSARY

culture: the beliefs and ways of life of a group of people

disband: to break up as a group

gourd: a fruit that has a hard shell and is used for decoration and not for eating

material: something used to make something else, such as cloth

museum: a building in which things of interest are displayed

primitive: made or done in a way that is not modern and that doesn't show skill. Also, coming from an early time.

professional: having to do with a job someone does for a living

religious: having to do with a belief in, and way of honoring, a god or gods

sacred: valued and important, usually in a religious way

symbol: a picture or shape that stands for something else

textile: a fabric or material that is woven or knit

traditional: having to do with long-practiced customs or ways of life

weaver: one who makes something by crossing threads or long material over and under each other

FOR MORE INFORMATION

BOOKS

Kavin, Kim. *Native Americans: Discover the History & Cultures of the First Americans*. White River Junction, VT: Nomad Press, 2013.

McNutt, Nan, and Bruce "Subiyay" Miller. *The Twined Basket: A Native American Art Activity Book*. Portland, OR: Westwinds Press, 2011.

Nolan, Mary. *Totem Poles and Masks: Art of Northwest Coast Tribes*. New York, NY: Rosen Classroom, 2013.

WEBSITES

American Indian Petroglyphs and Rock Paintings
singingdesert.com/
See examples of ancient rock paintings.

Legends and Symbology
shop.slcc.ca/legends-symbology/?q=/node/5
Click on these images for more facts about them.

Publisher's note to educators and parents: Our editors have carefully reviewed these websites to ensure that they are suitable for students. Many websites change frequently, however, and we cannot guarantee that a site's future contents will continue to meet our high standards of quality and educational value. Be advised that students should be closely supervised whenever they access the Internet.

INDEX